W9-CES-546

Great Scientists in Action

Early Life, Discoveries and Experiments

Written by Ed Shevick

Illustrated by Ron Wheeler

DISCARDED
from
New Hanover County Public Library

...aching & Learning Company

1204 Buchanan St., P.O. Box 10
Carthage, IL 62321-0010

NEW HANOVER COUNTY
PUBLIC LIBRARY
201 CHESTNUT STREET
WILMINGTON, NC 28401

This book belongs to

_____

Cover design by Sara King

Copyright © 2004, Teaching & Learning Company

ISBN No. 1-57310-436-1

Printing No. 987654321

Teaching & Learning Company
1204 Buchanan St., P.O. Box 10
Carthage, IL 62321-0010

The purchase of this book entitles teachers to make copies for use in their individual classrooms only. This book, or any part of it, may not be reproduced in any form for any other purposes without prior written permission from the Teaching & Learning Company. It is strictly prohibited to reproduce any part of this book for an entire school or school district, or for commercial resale.

All rights reserved. Printed in the United States of America.

Table of Contents

Dear Teacher or Parent,

This is a book about scientists in action. Each chapter begins with the early life of a scientist. Most were not privileged and had to struggle to succeed.

The middle of each chapter tells of their outstanding accomplishments. Each of them made discoveries that changed our world.

Each chapter concludes with one or more experiments that fit the scientist. For Galileo, students will work on gravity. For the Wright Brothers, students will fly paper airplanes.

All the experiments are "hands on." All are simply written with great graphics. The experiments use common, easily found materials.

This book tries to show scientists as human beings who achieved great things. Repeating their experiments helps young people relate to these science heroes. Hopefully, students will be encouraged to find their future in science.

Sincerely,

Ed

Ed Shevick

TLC10436 Copyright © Teaching & Learning Company, Carthage, IL 62321-0

Aristotle
An Observer of Nature

Born: 384 B.C. in Greece   Lived to be 62 years old

Young Aristotle

Science did not begin yesterday. Scientific thinking goes far back, even to prerecorded history and primitive people. When a person in ancient times tied a rock to a stick to make a weapon, he was thinking scientifically. The first farmer to discover that placing certain seeds in the ground would give rise to an edible plant was a scientist. Long ago people looked up at the stars and kept records of their path through the sky—they were the first astronomers.

Aristotle was among the first scientists to carefully observe nature. He wrote more than 150 books detailing what he learned about plants, animals and nature.

Aristotle was born to a wealthy family. His father was a doctor who served royalty. Young Aristotle learned much when he went with his dad to help the sick.

His dad died when Aristotle was only 10 years old. Since his mother was also dead, he was sent to live with a guardian.

At 17 Aristotle attended a school in Athens led by a genius named Plato. Plato was the most famous philosopher of his time. Aristotle soon became Plato's best student. Plato called him the "intelligence" of the school.

Aristotle stayed at the school for 20 years. He later started his own school. Most of his lectures were given outdoors as he and his students walked through the gardens of Athens.

Later in life Aristotle became a tutor to a young prince. He must have done a great job. The young prince grew up to be Alexander the Great.

Charles Darwin, a scientist in the nineteenth century, wrote that most scientists are mere "schoolboys" compared to Aristotle. What do you think he meant?

Why Aristotle Was Famous

Aristotle was a philosopher who thought and wrote about the meaning of life. He wrote books on logical thinking. He taught many of the most important people of his time.

Aristotle was also a scientist. He carefully observed and wrote about all things in nature. His books stressed that observation was an important part of science.

Aristotle did not have microscopes or telescopes. As a result he made many mistakes. His books are full of ideas that we now know are wrong such as:

1. Flies and worms are formed when fruit rots.

2. The only four elements in the world are earth, air, fire and water.

3. The job of the human brain is to cool off the body.

Aristotle's Favorite Experiments

Aristotle taught his students to observe carefully. Here are two optical illusions to challenge your observation power. Guess the answers, then measure to find out if you're right.

Which of the **center** circles is larger?

Which of the men is the tallest?

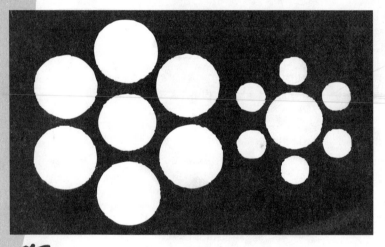

Aristotle taught logical thinking. Can you use your logical brain to solve the puzzles below?

1. What is the missing number in this series?

   24   20   _____   12   8   4

2. An archaeologist claims to have found a metal coin stamped 300 B.C. Why is this coin a fake?

3. A box is 10 feet long and 10 feet wide. It can hold 400 cubic feet. How deep is the box?

TLC10436 Copyright © Teaching & Learning Company, Carthage, IL 62321-00

Observing a Nickel

There were metal coins in Aristotle's time. He would have been amazed at our common nickel. Let's observe a nickel carefully.

- Obtain some shiny nickels.

- Observe the face on the coin. It is Thomas Jefferson.

- Observe the building on the back of the coin. It is Jefferson's mansion. Notice the name of the mansion right under it.

- Hold the nickel so that Jefferson's face is pointing up. Turn the coin to observe the mansion. It is upside down.

- Look for the word *liberty* to the right of the face. Notice the date when the coin was made.

- Look below the date. You may see a D or S. This stands for the location of the mint that made the coin. D is for Denver. S is for San Francisco. Those nickels without a letter were made in Philadelphia.

- Look above the mansion. You will see *E Pluribus Unum*. This is Latin. It means "one among many." This reflects the joining of the original 13 states.

Nickel Note: Did you know that some nickels are very valuable? A 1913 liberty head nickel can be worth more than a million dollars.

Observe and Draw

Sketch the two sides of a nickel. Look carefully, as if you were a student of Aristotle's. Show as many details as you can.

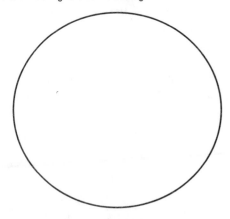

face

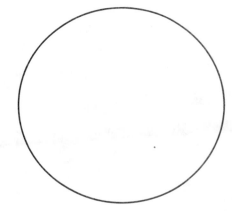

back side

Famous Quotes from Aristotle

Nature does nothing uselessly.

Well begun is half done.

Liars when they speak the truth are not believed.

LC10436 Copyright © Teaching & Learning Company, Carthage, IL 62321-0010

Galileo Galilei

Experimenter

Born: 1564 in Pisa, Italy   Lived to be 77 years old

Young Galileo

Try to imagine Pisa, Italy, where Galileo grew up. It was a small country town completely surrounded by a high wall. The center of the town was dominated by a 180-foot church tower. The builders of the tower made a mistake and the tower leaned sideways 15 feet at the top. It is still famous as the Leaning Tower of Pisa.

Young Galileo had no television, computer or movies. There were no cars or electric lights. His family came from nobility but had run out of money. His dad was a merchant and a musician.

Galileo showed an interest in toys and math. He learned how to play both the flute and the organ. He was also a very good painter. He showed early signs of the genius that he would become.

When Galileo was eight years old, his family moved to Florence, Italy, leaving him back in Pisa with a relative. At 15 he joined a monastery. He loved the peace and quiet of the monastery. After two years his dad pulled him out so he could begin studying to be a doctor at the University of Pisa.

Galileo did not like medicine. He thought it was boring compared to science and math. He was called the "wrangler" by his professors because he loved to argue. Galileo switched to math. He did so well that they made him a professor at the age of 25.

TLC10436 Copyright © Teaching & Learning Company, Carthage, IL 62321-001

Galileo and the Leaning Tower of Pisa

Over a thousand years before Galileo, Aristotle had written books on gravity. He claimed that a heavy object would fall faster than a light object. No one ever challenged Aristotle's theory until Galileo decided to do an experiment. He dropped a heavy and a light object from the Leaning Tower.

The experiment proved that Aristotle had been wrong. Aristotle was very smart, but he had never experimented, he merely thought about things. It took Galileo to make experiments an important part of the scientific method.

Try a dropping experiment of your own.

- Fill a small plastic water bottle half full of water.

- Fill a similar bottle one-fourth full of water.

- Close both lids tightly.

- Take a sturdy chair outside.

- Stand on the chair. Hold a bottle in each hand at the **same height**.

- Have a friend signal you when to drop both bottles at the **same time**. You should try this a few times to be sure the experiment was done right.

Describe what happened.

Who was right, Aristotle or Galileo?

Galileo got in trouble for his experiments with dropped objects. The other professors had taught the wrong idea for years. They resented this young man proving them wrong.

Why Galileo Was Famous

Most scientists before Galileo simply studied old textbooks or observed nature. Galileo tested his ideas with experiments to find out the truth. He is called the Father of Experimental Science. Here are some of Galileo's accomplishments.

1. He invented a weird, but working, thermometer.
2. He established laws of gravity and motion.
3. He vastly improved the telescope, though he did not invent it.

Galileo's Telescope

Galileo was also an astronomer. He turned his telescopes on the moon and discovered its rough surface. He found sunspots moving across the sun. He was the first person to spot the moons of Jupiter. He discovered that the Milky Way was made of millions of stars.

When Galileo was only 20, he went to pray at the cathedral one evening. He observed a worker lighting the candles on a big lamp which was attached by a chain to the ceiling. Galileo was fascinated by the lamp swinging back and forth. He observed that a small swing and a large swing of the lamp **took the same time**. He used his pulse to do the timing.

Galileo had discovered the law of the pendulum. He experimented to find that the only way to change the time of a pendulum was to change its length. Years later this principle would be used to build a pendulum clock.

A Pendulum Experiment

Pendulums are easy to build. All you need is string and some weights. Here are some suggestions for building a simple timing pendulum.

- You'll need: 5 feet of string, a ruler, a meterstick, some heavy metal washers and a clock or watch.

- Place a sturdy chair safely on a table.

- Place a ruler on the chair so that it extends beyond the table. Use a few books on top of the ruler to hold it steady.

- Tie some washers on one end of the string.

- Loosely tie the other end to the end of the ruler. Adjust the string so it is 40 inches (about 100 centimeters) from the pivot point of the string to the **center of the washer weights**.

- Pull the weight as far as you wish to one side. Have a friend count the number of swings in 60 seconds. A swing to the right is one swing. A swing back to the left is another swing.

TLC10436 Copyright © Teaching & Learning Company, Carthage, IL 62321-001

Try this experiment a few times. Record your swings in 60 seconds in the data table below.

Pendulum Data Table

Trial #	Swings in 60 Seconds
1	
2	
3	
4	
5	

You should now have a useful second timer. A pendulum of 40 inches (about 100 centimeters) length should give you a one-second swing. You may have to adjust your string length to get exactly one second. Shorten the string slightly to speed up your pendulum. Lengthen the string to slow it down.

Famous Quote from Galileo

We cannot teach people anything,
we can only help them discover it within themselves.

Isaac Newton
Scientific Laws

Born: 1642 in England   Lived to be 85 years old

Young Isaac Newton

Isaac was the son of a wealthy farmer who could not read or write. Isaac never knew him, because he died three months before Isaac was born.

His mother remarried when Isaac was only three. He never got along with his stepfather.

Isaac did not get off to a good start in school. His teachers described him as "idle and inattentive." They never dreamed he would become one of the world's greatest intellects.

Young Isaac was a serious, quiet child who rarely played with other children. He was not strong and avoided the rough games other children played.

He spent most of his time making model kites, sundials and wagons. He even made a windmill moved by a mouse running on a wheel.

It was lucky for Isaac that he had an uncle who recognized his genius. The uncle arranged for him to enter the famous Cambridge College. He was supposed to become a lawyer but, his interests were in math and science.

While Newton was in college, a terrible plague spread throughout England. The college was closed and Isaac spent over a year on his mother's farm. It turned out to be the most productive period in his life. He used the time to make brilliant discoveries in both math and science.

TLC10436 Copyright © Teaching & Learning Company, Carthage, IL 62321-001

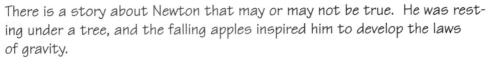

Why Newton Was Famous

There is a story about Newton that may or may not be true. He was resting under a tree, and the falling apples inspired him to develop the laws of gravity.

Aristotle had stressed **observation** in science. Galileo stressed **experimentation**. Newton went beyond observing and experimenting. He organized his discoveries into **laws** based on math.

Isaac Newton was a great mathematician who mastered all the math books he could find. He even invented a new math called calculus.

Newton loved astronomy. He built some of the finest telescopes of his day and invented a telescope that used mirrors instead of lenses to focus light. His studies of the heavens resulted in laws that explain the orbits of the planets.

Newton worked as a chemist, developing new kinds of metal alloys. This became important when later he was in charge of England's mint.

He astounded the world with his discovery that sunlight is made of all the colors of the rainbow. He invented a three-sided piece of glass called a prism to break sunlight into colors.

Here is how you can make your own rainbow using nature's method. Nature uses water drops suspended in air as prisms. That is why you often see a rainbow after a storm. For best results, do this experiment early in the morning or late in the afternoon.

- Spray water from a hose against a background of trees.
- Your **back** should be facing the sun.

With a little luck you should see a rainbow. Describe the colors that you see.

Newton's Laws of Motion

Newton developed three powerful laws to describe and predict how objects move. They explain the motion of the planets.

Law 1: This is often called the law of inertia. It says that an object at rest tends to stay at rest. An object in motion will tend to stay in motion.

- You'll need: a glass, a file card and a quarter.
- Place the card on the glass as shown.
- Place the coin on the card at the center of the glass.
- Use your finger to **quickly flick** the card across the top of the glass.

What happened to the quarter?

The quarter had inertia. It was at rest. It obeyed Newton's law and fell into the glass.

LC10436 Copyright © Teaching & Learning Company, Carthage, IL 62321-0010

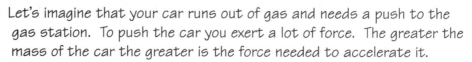

Law 2: This law explains the relationship between acceleration, mass and force.

This is not an easy law to understand.

You step into a car. It is not moving. As it starts and picks up speed we say that it is accelerating.

It is easier to accelerate a light car than a heavy truck. To scientists the "heaviness" is a measure of mass. A bowling ball would have more mass than a basketball.

Let's imagine that your car runs out of gas and needs a push to the gas station. To push the car you exert a lot of force. The greater the mass of the car the greater is the force needed to accelerate it.

Law 3: Action and reaction. This law is the basis for all rockets that fly into space. According to Newton, the gas leaving the rear of the rocket is the action. The reaction pushes the rocket into space.

- You'll need: a large balloon.

- Blow it up to the size of your head.

- Hold the neck tightly, raise it above your head and let it go.

The air coming out of the balloon was the action. The reaction was the weird flight of the balloon back to the ground.

Most of Isaac Newton's work in science and math was done before he was 25. He argued with other scientists, and delayed publishing his discoveries. He did admit how much he owed to the scientists before him such as Galileo.

Famous Quote from Newton

If I have seen further, it is from standing on the shoulders of giants.

TLC10436 Copyright © Teaching & Learning Company, Carthage, IL 62321-00

Benjamin Franklin
Scientist and Statesman

Born: January 17, 1706, in Boston, Massachusetts
Lived to be 84 years old

Young Benjamin Franklin

Ben Franklin was the fifteenth of seventeen children in his family. His parents were very poor. His father ran a small shop that made soap and candles.

Ben went to school for only two years, he left school to work in the family factory. Ben cut the wicks and melted the wax for candles.

At 12 he went to work at his brother's print shop. Printing in those days was hard, complicated work. Ben quickly became a master printer and an avid reader.

Ben loved to write. His brother James published a newspaper in Boston. He refused to publish any articles by his little brother. Ben wrote a story under a fake name. He pushed the article under the print shop door. His brother loved the writing and published it in his paper.

Tired of Boston at 17, Ben ran away to Philadelphia. He arrived with only a dollar and three loaves of bread.

Why Franklin Was Famous

Ben had many talents. He started his own print shop and later published his own newspaper. He also published a yearly almanac that helped farmers and other people plan their lives. The almanac was full of his witty comments.

Franklin established the first library in Philadelphia. He helped start the postal service in Pennsylvania.

He made important contributions to our nation's Constitution and the Declaration of Independence. He also served as ambassador to France during the American Revolution.

LC10436 Copyright © Teaching & Learning Company, Carthage, IL 62321-0010

Curious about the world of nature, Franklin was a scientist and inventor.

1. He made a musical instrument out of water-filled glasses.
2. He invented a wood-burning stove. The design of the stove is still used today.
3. He made a measuring device that attached to a horse and buggy. It told the distance the wagon traveled.
4. He invented bifocal glasses that enabled people to see both near and far.
5. He designed one of the first electric batteries.
6. He developed a lightning rod that kept buildings from catching fire during electrical storms.

Franklin's Favorite Experiment

On a stormy June day, Ben and his son William decided to do an experiment. They wanted to find out if lightning was made of electricity.

They flew a kite up high in the rainstorm. William flew the kite. Ben attached a large brass key near the end of the string. Ben placed a finger near the key. A spark jumped to his hand. This showed that lightning is electricity.

Caution! Do **not** try this experiment; it is very **dangerous**! Franklin was lucky not to get hurt!

More Franklin Experiments

Ben loved to tinker with electricity. Here is a simple battery you can make:

• You'll need: a lemon, a shiny penny and a dime.
• Have an adult cut grooves for the coins in the side of the lemon. They should be about 1/2 inch apart and deep enough to hold half of the coins.
• Place the penny in one groove and the dime in the other groove.
• Squeeze the lemon to get the most juice on the coins. The lemon acid causes electricity to flow between the different coin metals.
• Stick out your tongue and place both coins on it. Do you feel the tingle of electricity? Don't worry, it's safe!

TLC10436 Copyright © Teaching & Learning Company, Carthage, IL 62321-00

Here are some simpler and safer experiments you can do with static electricity:

- You'll need: a large balloon, some light string and a piece of fur or wool cloth.

- Blow the balloon to the size of your face.

- Tie the mouth of the balloon into a knot to keep the air in.

- Rub the balloon **vigorously** with the fur or wool. Quickly place the balloon near, but not touching, your ear. You should feel and hear the spark.

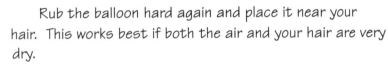

- Rub the balloon hard again and place it near your hair. This works best if both the air and your hair are very dry.

- Tie 12 inches of light string to the mouth of the balloon. Rub the balloon hard.

- Have a friend hold the end of the string. Bring your hand slowly near the balloon. Describe what happens.

- Adjust a water faucet to get a very slow drip. Rub the balloon and bring it near, but not touching, the water drops. Describe what happens.

Famous Quotes from Franklin

Ben Franklin was as great a writer as he was a scientist. Below are some famous quotes from his almanac.

Eat to live, and not live to eat.

Early to bed and early to rise, makes a man healthy, wealthy and wise.

He who lies down with dogs shall rise up with fleas.

Little strokes fell great oaks.

A penny saved is a penny earned.

Haste makes waste.

Pick your favorite among these Franklin quotes. Try to explain in detail what he meant. Write a "quote" of your own. Maybe it will make you famous.

TLC10436 Copyright © Teaching & Learning Company, Carthage, IL 62321-0010

Charles Darwin

Evolution Scientist

Born: 1809 in Shrewsbury, England   Lived to be 73 years old

Young Charles Darwin

Charles Darwin was the fifth child and second son of a wealthy physician. His dad was a huge man who was over six feet tall and weighed more than 300 pounds. Charles was in awe of his father all his life.

His mother was a sickly woman who died when he was only eight years old.

Young Darwin disliked school. His teachers called him "just ordinary in intellect." They were wrong.

Charles preferred hunting and fishing to school. He collected and brought home rocks, fish, plants, shells and insects. Collecting was his hobby and passion.

One day Charles spotted three rare beetles. He put one in his mouth and one in each fist to carry them home. We don't know if he made it home with all the beetles alive.

At 16 Darwin was sent to Edinburgh University in Scotland. His father wanted him to become a doctor. After seeing blood in his surgery class, Darwin decided that medicine was not for him. Instead he studied to be a minister.

TLC10436 Copyright © Teaching & Learning Company, Carthage, IL 62321-0010

Darwin's Accomplishments

Did anything ever happen to you that changed your life?

Darwin's luck began when he was 22. He was invited to sail around the world on an English navy scientific expedition.

He embarked on the *HMS Beagle* for an almost five-year journey around the world. The ship had three masts, 10 guns, carried 74 passengers and was 85 feet long.

Darwin spent his time collecting and observing rocks, plants and animals. He observed and collected data on everything in sight.

Back home in England, Darwin spent 20 years studying his specimens and his notes. He finally wrote a book called *On the Origins of the Species*. The book shook up the scientific world.

Darwin's theories were about **evolution**. *Evolution* means "evolving or changing." Here is a brief summary of his theory:

- Both plants and animals have more offspring than are needed for reproduction.

- The offspring may differ slightly from their parents. A type of butterfly could have a more colorful wing to help it attract a mate.

- Plants and animals struggle to survive. The world is full of enemies. (Grasshoppers may love to eat a particular plant's leaves and eventually destroy it.)

- Those plants and animals that survive are the most fit. (Young wolves that are faster than their parents have a better chance to survive.)

Let's explore a few examples of Darwin's theory of survival of the fittest.

Observe the snowshoe rabbits in winter and summer. How does being white in winter help the rabbit survive?

Observe the long-necked giraffe. How does being tall help them feed?

Observe the feet of a duck and a hawk. Explain what each type of foot is adapted to do.

Duck's Foot

Hawk's Foot

Survival of the Cereal Bug

Insects vary in color. The colors can help an insect find a mate or scare off an enemy. Use a common colorful cereal to find which cereal bugs survive near you.

- You'll need: some Post® Fruity Pebbles (or similar) cereal. They will be your cereal bugs.

- Pick out 10 of each color.

- Find a grassy area under a tree where birds are likely to be.

- Mark off a six-foot square area.

- Spread the cereal bugs evenly over the area.

- Wait a day to give birds a chance to find the cereal bugs.

- Pick up all the cereal bugs that you can find and fill out the data table below.

Cereal Bug Data Table

Colors	Example	Red	Green	Orange	Yellow	Purple	Blue
Original Bug Totals	10	10	10	10	10	10	10
Bugs You Found	3						
Missing Bugs	7						

Which cereal bug color had the most survivors?

Which cereal bug color had the least survivors?

Explain what happened in terms of Darwin's theory.

Famous Quote from Darwin

I love fool's experiments. I am always making them.

TLC10436 Copyright © Teaching & Learning Company, Carthage, IL 62321-0010

Louis Pasteur

Bacteriologist

Born: 1822 in Dole, France   Lived to be 72 years old

Young Louis Pasteur

Louis Pasteur's father was a peasant who had served in Napoleon's army.
He made a living tanning leather in his home.

Young Louis did not start out as a genius. He was a slow student who cared more for fishing than studying.

His early talent was in art. Pasteur loved to paint portraits. Some of his later paintings are in museums.

At 15 one of his teachers became impressed with his intellect. He encouraged Louis to go to Paris and study for college entrance exams. Louis followed his advice and went to Paris. He quickly became homesick, and his dad came to take him back to their village.

Louis studied at home for a year. He passed the exams and eventually ended up in the famous Sorbonne University in Paris. There he studied both chemistry and biology.

Why Pasteur Was Famous

Pasteur was among the most famous scientists of his day. At the age of 25 he became famous for experiments on crystals.

His gift was combining imagination with experiments. Pasteur applied science principles to solve problems in industry and medicine.

TLC10436 Copyright © Teaching & Learning Company, Carthage, IL 62321-0010

Here are some of his discoveries:

Bacteria and Disease

Pasteur discovered the connection between bacteria and disease. He learned how to grow and control bacteria.

Spontaneous Generation of Life

Uneducated people saw roaches and flies coming out of garbage. They assumed that filth created life. They called that spontaneous generation. Pasteur's experiments showed that living things could only come from other living things.

Pasteurization

Pasteur's experiments helped both the dairy and wine industries. Take a look at most milk cartons. They probably say "Pasteurized." Pasteur learned that milk could be made safer by a quick heating and cooling that killed most harmful bacteria.

Rabies

Rabies is a dangerous disease spread by the bite of infected animals. Rabies was a serious problem in Pasteur's time. He experimented to find a vaccine that could fight rabies.

Pasteur was once approached by a frantic father whose young son had been bitten by a rabid dog. The vaccine he was working on had not been tested on humans. He knew it was unwise, even dangerous, to give an untested vaccine.

But the father insisted, so Pasteur gave the boy the vaccine. The boy recovered and spent his adult years working for Dr. Pasteur.

Fermentation

Wine is very important in France. It is the national drink. At one time, the wine industry was threatened by bacteria that spoiled the wine. A call went out to Pasteur. He saved the wine industry and became even more of a national hero.

Wine is produced by a process called fermentation. The process uses yeast cell plants to produce the alcohol. Yeast cells grow best when placed in warm water with sugar or starches. As the yeast cells grow and divide, they give off alcohol. They also give off a gas called carbon dioxide. That is the gas that causes bread dough to rise.

Let's imitate Pasteur's yeast experiments.

- You'll need: some yeast, some sugar and a small baby food jar.

- Add a ½ inch of **warm** water to the jar.

- Add a level teaspoon of yeast.

- Add a heaping teaspoon of sugar.

- Stir the mixture and place it in a **warm, dark** place.

- Wait a few hours.

Observe the mixture. You should see bubbles. What gas is the yeast making?

TLC10436 Copyright © Teaching & Learning Company, Carthage, IL 62321-0010

A Bacteria Experiment

Pasteur was a bacteria expert. Here is a simple experiment you can do with bacteria:

- You'll need: a potato and four small plastic bags that zip up.

- Cut the potato into four circular slices about ¼- to ½-inch thick.

- Place a finger in dirt and rub it around. Place the dirty finger in the center of one slice and press down. Put the slice into a plastic bag and label it *dirt*. Seal the bag.

- Place hairs from various people on a second slice. Press the hairs into the slice with a clean toothpick. Place it in a bag. Label it *hair* and seal the bag.

- Place some of your saliva on a third slice. Rub it in with a fresh clean toothpick. Place it in a bag marked *saliva*.

- Place nothing on the fourth slice. It will be your **control**. Scientists use controls to compare their experiments.

- Handle the control slice by the edge. You don't want to contaminate the surface of the control slice. Place it in a bag, seal it and mark it *control*.

- Place all four sealed bags in a box. Place the covered box in a warm, dark place.

- Wait a few days.

Caution! From here on, **do not** open the sealed bags. They could contain harmful bacteria. Have an adult dispose of the bags when you are done observing.

Observation Time

Describe what you observe in each bag.

dirty finger bag

hair bag

saliva bag

control bag

Famous Quotes from Pasteur

Can you explain what Pasteur meant in your own words?

Chance favors the prepared mind.

Do not put forward anything that you cannot prove by experimentation.

Gregor Mendel

Heredity Scientist

Born: 1822 in Heinzendorf, Austria   Lived to be 61 years old

Young Gregor Mendel

Gregor's parents were peasant farmers. As a child, Gregor worked on the farm. He did not go to school until he was 11.

Going to school was not easy for a peasant's son. Everyone in the family had to sacrifice to send Gregor to school. His sacrifice was to eat only half of a normal meal.

Despite such hardships, Mendel did brilliantly in school. There was no money for college. Instead, Gregor joined a monastery where he was sent to college to become a teacher. He failed at teacher's college. His worst grades were in biology, studying living things. The failed student would eventually become a world-famous biologist.

Mendel was lucky in his choice of a monastery. It had large gardens with a variety of plants. The abbot (person in charge) was science oriented and encouraged all his monks to experiment. Years later, Mendel became abbot of the monastery.

Why Mendel Was Famous

Mendel's first experiments were with flowers. He tried to cross plants to get new colors.

Most of his experiments were with pea plants. He grew almost 30,000 pea plants in his lifetime, trying to discover how pea plant characteristics were passed from generation to generation.

Pea plants can be very different. Some are tall and some are short. Some have green peas and some have yellow peas. Some peas are smooth and some are wrinkled.

TLC10436 Copyright © Teaching & Learning Company, Carthage, IL 62321-001

Mendel crossed different kinds of pea plants. He discovered that each pea plant trait had **two factors** involved. One factor could **dominate** and show up in new plants. The other factor was **recessive** and may not show up right away.

Mendel's experiments found that tall plants were dominant over small plants. Smooth peas were dominant over wrinkled peas. Yellow peas were dominant over green peas.

When different pea plants were crossed, each parent gave **only one** factor to the new plant. Tall plants crossed with a short plant gave rise to the dominant tall plant. If you crossed smooth peas with wrinkled peas, the smooth pea was dominant.

Mendel had discovered the basic laws of **heredity**. Heredity deals with how characteristics are passed from one generation to another. Mendel was lucky. Pea plant factors were simple. Many living things have more complicated heredity factors. What Mendel called factors are now known as **genes**.

Gregor Mendel published his findings in an obscure science journal in 1866. He died in 1884. His paper was ignored until it was rediscovered in 1900. He became famous years after his death.

Scientists like Mendel often work with many unknown factors. His work involved genes, but he never knew about or saw a gene. Here is an experiment with vegetable colors that will help you see what is normally hidden.

- You'll need: two different colors of vegetable dyes, a paper cup, a tall glass and a paper towel.

- Mix three drops of each color together in the paper cup.

- Fill the glass one-third full of water.

- Cut a strip of paper towel so that is it 1" x 8" long.

- Place the paper strip as shown into the glass. The top should be bent around the glass edge.

- Add a single drop of your vegetable dye mixture at a point on the paper an inch above the water level as shown.

- Wait a few minutes, then answer the question below.

You are doing an experiment called chromatography. As the water rises in the paper strip, the different colors will separate. List all the colors you see.

What color traveled the farthest on the paper strip? _____
That color had the lightest molecule.

What color traveled the least on the paper strip? _____
That color had the heaviest molecule.

Human Heredity

Human heredity is more complicated than pea plant heredity. Each human cell has 23 pairs of **chromosomes**. Chromosomes are made up of much smaller particles called genes.

Let's compare some of your characteristics with those of your family. Don't take the results too seriously. Humans can differ widely.

Compare these family traits.

1. Eye color: Yours: _____   Your family: _____
   _____

2. Hair color: Yours: _____   Your family: _____
   _____

3. Hair texture—curly or straight:
   Yours: _____   Your family: _____
   _____

4. Ear lobe—free or attached:
   Yours: _____   Your family: _____
   _____

5. Tongue—ability to curl:
   Yours: _____   Your family: _____
   _____

6. Hair whorl—clockwise or counterclockwise:
   Yours: _____   Your family: _____
   _____

Poetry Time

Complete this poem with three lines of information that you learned in this chapter.

There was a monk named Gregor

Famous Quote from Mendel

It is just a little trick, but there is a long story connected with it . . .

(to C.W. Eichling)

TLC10436 Copyright © Teaching & Learning Company, Carthage, IL 62321-00

Thomas Alva Edison

Inventor

Born: 1847 in Milan, Ohio   Lived to be 84 years old

Young Thomas Edison

Tom was the youngest of seven children. He started school at age seven, but school was not easy for Tom. The other children teased him. His teacher called him "addled" which means "mixed up."

Tom ran away from school. In his entire life Edison only spent three months in a classroom. His mother taught him at home, introducing Tom to chemistry and science experiment books.

Young Tom was curious about everything. After he saw a goose sitting on eggs to hatch them, his mother found him sitting on eggs.

Tom was mischievous. He fell into a canal and nearly drowned. He once rubbed two cats together to see if an electric spark would jump between them.

Young Tom had gifted hands. He built many things including a steam engine train that hissed, rattled and sometimes exploded.

Edison was deaf most of his life. He once said that he hadn't heard a bird sing since he was 12 years old. In some ways he liked being deaf because it helped him concentrate on his experiments.

Children worked hard in those days. At 12 Tom was selling candy and newspapers on trains. He got up at 6 in the morning and didn't get home until 12 at night.

Why Edison Was Famous

Edison had over 1000 inventions to his name. The most famous was the electric light. Edison also invented a talking doll, an electric pen, a coal miner's safety lamp and the electric vacuum cleaner.

Many of Edison's inventions improved other devices. He invented the carbon microphone that made telephones sound better. He improved the automobile electric storage battery. He improved both the typewriters and cameras of his day.

Do you enjoy listening to music? Can you guess who invented the phonograph?

Do you appreciate having electricity in your home? Can you guess who first built the
generators, switches and lights to wire a city?

Edison even stumbled on something called the Edison Effect. It was the beginning of radio. It was left to other inventors to develop radio further.

Do you like movies? Edison invented the motion picture camera. He even made the first very primitive movies.

The movies are based upon fooling your eyes. If you show someone more than 20 pictures in a second, the eyes blend them into motion. The drawing below will prove how easily your eyes can be fooled into seeing motion.

- Hold the drawing about eight inches in front of your eyes.

- Stare at the center dot.

- **Keep the paper still**. Move your head only toward and away from the drawing while staring at the dot.

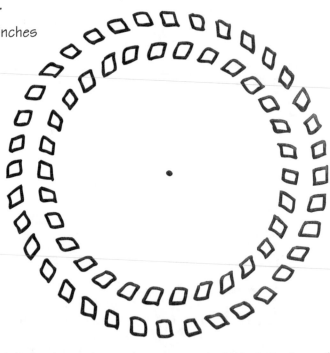

You should see the inner circle in motion. This is an optical illusion.

Edison invented the **incandescent** light bulb. Incandescent means so hot that it gives off light. Our sun is incandescent. So are the filaments (wires) in a light bulb.

Many scientists before Edison knew that hot wires give off light, but their wires quickly burned out. Edison spent two years trying to find a filament that would be bright and not burn out. He sent people searching all over the world. He tried thousands of materials. The answer came with ordinary cotton thread that he turned to carbon.

TLC10436 Copyright © Teaching & Learning Company, Carthage, IL 62321-00

Modern incandescent lights last for years. They use Tungsten as the filament. The air is partially removed and a gas called Argon is added. This keeps the glass from turning dark.

Take a good look at an **unlit** light bulb. Try to find the parts shown in the drawing.

Modern Incandescent Light Bulb

Clear or frosted glass

Incandescent filament (wire)

Partial vacuum—added argon gas

Base

Your Favorite Invention

Edison's invention changed people's lives. Imagine living without electricity, lights and movies.

Many other important inventions have changed your life. Below is a partial list.

- Study the list.

- Pick out one that interests you.

- Write a short paper explaining why that invention is so important.

- Share your report with others.

automobile	microwave oven	plastics	air conditioning
airplane	movie	nylon	radar
computer	telephone	antibiotics	contact lenses
paper	television	refrigerator	microscope
radio	elevator	copy machine	
camera	Scotch™ tape	light bulb	

The Invention Challenge

No one is sure who invented the paper clip. It is a simple but useful device. Post-It® notes invented by the 3M company now come in all colors, sizes and shapes.

Can you invent something useful? Perhaps a hammer that can be held in both hands. How about a better toothbrush or comb? Think of something at home or school that needs improvement.

- Imagine your invention.

- Sketch how it might look.

- Build a simple model of your invention.

- Demonstrate it to your family and friends.

Famous Quotes from Edison

Genius is 1% inspiration and 99% perspiration.

There are no rules. Here we try to accomplish something.

LC10436 Copyright © Teaching & Learning Company, Carthage, IL 62321-0010

George Washington Carver

Plant Doctor

Born: 1864 in Diamond, Missouri   Lived to be 78 years old

Young George Washington Carver

George Washington Carver was born a slave on a farm belonging to Moses Carver. His father died before his birth. Carver was a baby when he and his mother were kidnapped. His owner gave a horse to ransom them. The kidnappers returned baby George but not his mother. He never saw her again.

Young Carver was a weak child, so Mr. Moses let him do easy jobs in the house and garden. George was fascinated by plants. He became an expert, soon people were bringing him sick plants to heal. They called George the "plant doctor."

The first book he read was a spelling book. He memorized it from front to back. George taught himself to read and write.

He left the farm when he was 10. He worked his way through various high schools.

It was difficult for an African American to get into college in those days. George became the first of his race to be admitted to Iowa State College. He studied agriculture and mechanics.

Carver loved college. He joined the YMCA and the debate club. He worked in the dining room and the gym to pay for college.

Carver was an outstanding student, encouraged to get higher degrees specializing in plant breeding. He became the first African American on the Iowa State faculty.

Most of his career was spent at Tuskegee University in Alabama. His work there made him famous worldwide. Carver never married, he considered his students his children. He lived a very simple life.

TLC10436 Copyright © Teaching & Learning Company, Carthage, IL 62321-00

Why Carver Was Famous

Carver was a farmer's scientist. He showed farmers how to grow better plants, and he found uses even for farm waste products. Carver turned corn stalks into building materials. He found dyes in the rich clay soil. He made over 100 products from sweet potatoes. His favorite plant was the peanut. He discovered more than 300 ways to use the peanut. Through his genius, peanuts became soap, plastic, shampoo and even shoe polish.

Carver never patented any of his ideas. He felt that he should not profit from any discovery that God led him to make.

More about peanuts:

1. The average American eats three pounds of peanuts per year.

2. One acre of peanuts can make 30,000 sandwiches.

3. Two U.S. Presidents were peanut farmers—Thomas Jefferson and Jimmy Carter.

Carver developed many kinds of peanut butter. Here is an easy recipe for peanut butter that you can make:

- You'll need: a cup of roasted, unsalted, shelled peanuts, peanut oil and some salt.

- Add 1¹/₂ teaspoons of the oil to the cup of nuts.

- Add ¹/₄ teaspoon of salt.

- Mix in a blender for about four minutes. Add more oil as needed to make it smooth enough to spread.

- Place it in a covered jar in the refrigerator.

- Enjoy, but eat within two weeks.

Peanuts are not really nuts. They belong to the legume family with peas and beans.

Try being a peanut farmer.

- Obtain some raw peanuts. Many stores carry them in the produce section.

- Obtain a six-inch flowerpot with a bottom hole for drainage.

- Find some loose, sandy soil.

- Fill the pot with soil to within an inch of the top.

- Soak four healthy looking shelled peanuts overnight in water.

- Plant the nuts about an inch deep in the soil.

- Keep the soil moist but don't drown your seeds.

- When they sprout in about a week, place the flowerpot in bright sunlight.

- Add water as needed.

- Peanut plants take a few months to develop. Enjoy your plant, but don't expect a big harvest.

Don't look for your peanuts above ground. The nuts form underground with the roots.

Peanut Fun

Find some peanuts still in their shells. Pick out three with interesting, but different, shapes.

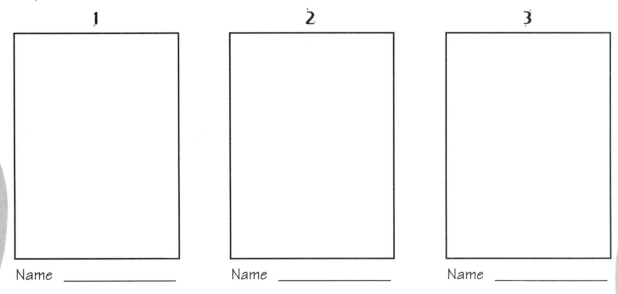

1

2

3

Name _____

Name _____

Name _____

- Draw or outline the peanuts in the boxes above.

- Give each peanut a suitable name. The size, shape or color might help. Peanuts in the shell can look as different as your friends do.

Imagination Time

- Decorate your three peanut friends. Glue paper arms, legs or heads on them. Color them or make clothes for them. Give the decorated peanuts to family or friends as gifts.

TLC10436 Copyright © Teaching & Learning Company, Carthage, IL 62321-00

Carver Invention Time

Carver discovered many uses for peanut shells. Can you do the same? Shells could be emptied and used to store water or jelly. Could you convert the shells into paper? Could you create a shell game?

Have fun with this project. Write your plans and results below.

Famous Quotes from Carver

Know science and science will set you free. Science is truth.

Look about you. Take hold of the things that are here.
Let them talk to you. Learn to talk to them.

C10436 Copyright © Teaching & Learning Company, Carthage, IL 62321-0010

Marie Curie

Pioneer Woman Scientist

Born: 1867 in Warsaw, Poland   Lived to be 66 years old

Young Marie Curie

Marie was the youngest of five children. Her father was a professor of math and physics. Her mother was a gifted musician.

Her maiden name was Sklodowska. Later she married a French scientist and took his last name, Curie.

Marie's mother died when she was only 10. Her dad read classic literature to his children and let them play with his science equipment.

Marie graduated at 15, then ran into a problem. Poland did not allow girls to go to college. Then her sister Bronya had an opportunity to go to Paris to become a doctor. Marie put her own future on hold to earn the money to support her sister's studies. She spent six years working as a tutor and governess.

Marie was 24 before it became her turn to go to Paris. She was admitted into the famous Sorbonne University. As a student she was very poor and lived in a cold attic, often with only bread and tea for food.

Why Curie Was Famous

Marie Curie was a pioneer for women's rights. She earned degrees in both math and physics and became famous all over the world.

She won two Nobel Prizes. Her first was for physics in 1903 for the discovery of radiation. She shared the prize with her husband. In 1911 she won her second Nobel Prize, this time in chemistry for isolating the atom, radium. She was the first person, male or female, to win twice.

TLC10436 Copyright © Teaching & Learning Company, Carthage, IL 62321-00

Her daughter, Irene, later also won a Nobel Prize for chemistry.

Marie began working in Paris, in her future husband's lab, at the Sorbonne University. The university had been in existence for 650 years, but a woman had never been a professor. Can you guess who became the first woman professor at the Sorbonne?

The radium that Marie Curie discovered became an early tool in fighting cancer. She was honored in 1921 with an invitation to the White House from President Harding. He presented her with a gram of radium. (A gram of radium weighs less than a penny, but it is more valuable than gold.)

A Mixture Separation Experiment

Marie and her husband spent years working with an ore called pitchblende. Pitchblende contains the heaviest atom called uranium. The Curie's were sure that other radioactive atoms were in the ore.

They were right. The ore contained two new atoms. One was radium, the other they named Polonium after her native country, Poland.

Separating the ore took the Curies years of work. Here are some simple separation experiments to challenge you. Look at the list below of strange mixtures. How would you separate them? You may need to experiment to decide. Keep a written record of your experiments and the results.

Example: How would you separate a mixture of sugar and salt? Place some ants on the mixture. They would carry away the sugar and leave the salt.

Separate these mixtures:

1. Sand and salt

2. Salt and iron filings

3. Sand and 1/4-inch pebbles

4. Sand and rice cereal

5. Salt and water

6. Dirt and water

7. Oil and water

8. Any mixture of your choice

A Fluorescent Experiment

Marie Curie invented the word *radioactivity*. It described particles being emitted from certain rocks.

Do this experiment to simulate radioactivity. (Real radioactive rocks are too dangerous to use.)

Leaves are green because they contain a dye called **chlorophyll**. The dye gets "excited" when struck by light. Electrons jump off the dye and emit a fluorescent light.

You'll need: a clear alcohol, a small baby food jar, a teaspoon, a small test tube and a strong flashlight.

- Find some dark green leaves.

- Crush them as much as possible with a teaspoon. Put them in the jar.

- Add enough alcohol to just cover the leaves.

- Cover the jar and shake for a full minute.

  - Wait 20 minutes and then shake again.

Your alcohol should now have a greenish color. That is the chlorophyll dye.

  - Pour the alcohol **only** into the small test tube.

  - Go to the darkest place that you can find.

  - Shine the flashlight under the test tube. Look through the side of the tube.

Observation Time

- You should see the green fluid glow. You may also see a reddish glow as the light knocks electrons off the dye.

Famous Quotes from Curie

Nothing in life is to be feared. It is only to be understood.

One never notices what has been done, one can only see what remains to be done.

TLC10436 Copyright © Teaching & Learning Company, Carthage, IL 62321-0

Wright Brothers
Aviation Pioneers

Wilbur

Born: 1867 in Millville, Indiana
Lived to be 45 years old

Orville

Born: 1871 in Dayton, Ohio
Lived to be 77 years old

The Early Years

Wilbur was four years older than Orville. The boys bonded early and did everything together. Neither ever married.

Their father was a minister. Both of their parents were well educated. Their home had a library full of books on literature and science. Both boys were avid readers, but neither of them finished high school.

Toys were plentiful in the Wright house. One of their early toys was a gyroscope with spinning wheels. Their favorite toy was a paper and wood helicopter. They wore it out, then built a better one on their own.

Their parents encouraged them to become independent. They were paid pennies to wash dishes, shovel snow, chop wood and clean chimneys.

Both boys loved flying kites and they became so good at it, they designed and sold their own kites. Orville was only 10 years old at the time.

At 15 Orville opened his own print shop. Soon he was publishing a weekly newspaper. Later the boys teamed up to open a bicycle shop. They rented, repaired and sold bikes. They even manufactured their own bikes.

It took mechanical skills to run a bike shop. Years later they used these same skills, and some bike parts, to build their airplanes.

Why the Wright Brothers Were Famous

The Wright brothers were awarded the Congressional Medal of Honor in 1909. The world showered them with awards.

They were not the first to try to fly. They were the first to fly a **controlled** plane over a distance.

Their skill as bicycle mechanics helped them build their planes. They also read every book they could find about flying. They tested their early ideas with kites. They later built one of the first wind tunnels to test wings and controls.

The first models were only 16 feet wide and cost $15 to build. Their successful plane was 40 feet wide, weighed 750 pounds (including the pilot) and cost $1000. The light gasoline engine on the plane was designed and built by the brothers.

The date was December 17, 1903. The place was Kitty Hawk, North Carolina, picked for being windy. The brothers tossed a coin to decide who would pilot the plane. Orville won and flew into the history books.

Here is a way for you to understand how short the first flight was.

- Use a watch to measure out the short 12 seconds of the flight. Your heart may have beat 15 times in the 12 seconds.

- Measure and mark off 120 feet. That was the distance of the first flight. It is a little over one third of a football field.

- Time how long it takes you to run the 120 feet.

Congratulations! You probably ran faster than the first plane.

TLC10436 Copyright © Teaching & Learning Company, Carthage, IL 62321-00

Birds in Motion

People have always envied birds because they soar in the sky while we are stuck on the ground. Early inventors tied wings to their arms and tried to flap their way into the sky. It took the Wright brothers to show that flight was possible.

Birds are built to fly. Their bones and parts of their bodies are hollow. Feathers adjust to help them soar and glide. Powerful wings flap in complicated patterns.

Watch some birds in motion. Find an area with trees and birds. A pair of binoculars will help you see them better. Large birds are easier to observe in flight.

Bird-watching is a popular hobby. People watch birds to identify them by size, shape, color, beak or claw.

Concentrate on birds in motion. Try to observe how birds take off, fly and land. Landing on a narrow twig is a very athletic feat.

The flight pictures may help you. Observe carefully and write down six new things that you learn about bird motion.

1. _____

2. _____

3. _____

4. _____

5. _____

6. _____

LC10436 Copyright © Teaching & Learning Company, Carthage, IL 62321-0010

A Paper Airplane Flying Contest

To make a simple paper airplane, start with a sheet of standard notebook paper. Follow the instructions below carefully. It may take a few tries to get it right. Compete with friends to see who can fly their planes the farthest in a long hall or an outdoor spot with little wind.

- Fold the paper in half the long way.
- Fold the two top edges into the center as shown in figure A.
- Press hard to flatten the folds.
- Fold the first folds inward toward the center line as shown in figure B. Press the edges. Your plane should now look like figure C.
- Fold it **upward** at the center line away from the previous folds. Press the fold.
- Place one staple in the center of the plane about ½ inch from the bottom. See figure D.
- Adjust the wings so that they are at right angles to the stapled section as shown in figure E.
- Write your name on your plane, and color it with a special design.
- Press down on all the folds. Adjust the wings so that they are level.
- Practice throwing your plane. It works best if tilted slightly upward.
- Compete for distance with your friends. Mark the best of three throws as your entry.

Have fun. Try to go farther than the Wright brothers' first plane.

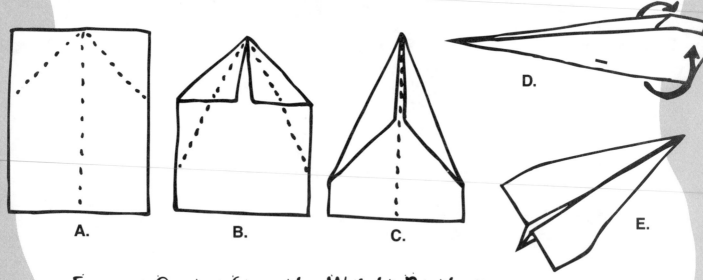

A.   B.   C.   D.   E.

Famous Quotes from the Wright Brothers

We were lucky enough to grow up in a home where there was encouragement to investigate anything that aroused curiosity.

At the time we flew our first plane, we were not thinking of any practical uses at all. We just wanted to show that it was possible to fly.

TLC10436 Copyright © Teaching & Learning Company, Carthage, IL 62321-001

Albert Einstein

Math Genius

Born: 1879 in Germany   Lived to be 76 years old

Young Albert Einstein

Albert Einstein was a math genius who won a Nobel Prize, but, there was little in his early years to predict what he would become.

Albert's parents worried because he hardly spoke before the age of three. At age five, he became very sick. His parents brought him a compass. Albert tried as hard as he could to keep it from pointing north. This started his curiosity about all things in nature.

At age six, Albert learned to play the violin. Music became his lifelong passion.

Albert disliked school, especially the rules. He was shy and preferred to be alone. He did so poorly that he once dropped out of school.

At age 12, someone gave him a geometry book. He was fascinated by the math. His mind was made to solve math problems. This was the start of his math career.

Why Einstein Was Famous

Einstein did not do experiments. He did not have a lab, equipment or even a computer. His tools were pen and paper or chalk on a board. His discoveries began and ended as math equations.

It is not easy for an average person to understand Einstein's work. His equations predicted that light could be bent by massive objects in space. Astronomers soon proved that his predictions were right.

One of his theories involved the speed of light and space travel. He imagined a pair of twins on Earth. One went on a long space journey traveling at almost the speed of light. The other twin stayed on Earth. Einstein predicted that the returned space traveler would be younger than his brother.

Einstein worked on the math of what he called the "photoelectric" effect. This led to the development of solar cells that turn light energy into electricity.

Einstein's equations led to an explanation of something called the Brownian Movement. This involves small particles in motion in a liquid or gas. Do this a simple experiment to help you understand Brownian Movement.

- You'll need: a glass and some **dark** vegetable dye.

- Add **warm** water till the glass is three-fourths full.

- Place a few drops of dye into the water.

Observe what happens. In a short time the dye is evenly distributed all through the water. The water molecules are in constant motion. They push the dye around.

Energy, Mass and Velocity

Einstein is especially famous for this formula: **$E = MC^2$**.

The formula looks simple. It was the result of years of work by Einstein. It is much more complicated than it looks. It says that energy can be converted to matter and that matter can be converted to energy. The atom bomb came out of this equation. So does the atomic energy that makes electricity for our homes.

The **E** stands for **energy**. Scientists measure this energy in units called **joules**.

The **M** stands for **mass**. The unit is the **kilogram**.

The **C** stands for **velocity**. Velocity is the speed of light measured in **meters per second**. The velocity of light is about 300 million meters per second. At that speed, light can travel from the moon to Earth in a little over one second.

TLC10436 Copyright © Teaching & Learning Company, Carthage, IL 62321-001

Fun with Math

Einstein would have enjoyed these math problems. The answers are on page 64.

1. How many blocks are there in each of these stacks?

Left Block

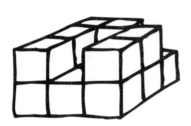

Right Block

2. Fill in the square to the right. Each three spaces should add up to 15. This is for spaces up and down, left and right and diagonal.

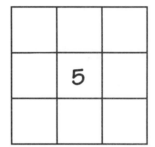

3. Digital watches give their numbers in a series of lines. To the right is a math equation that is wrong. Can you move only one line and make the equation right?

$$12 - 3 = 19$$

Einstein in America

In 1933 Albert Einstein had to flee Nazi Germany. He came to America and spent the rest of his life working at Princeton University.

He was admired by everyone for his wit and modesty. He would sit for hours on a park bench helping young students with their science projects.

Imagination Time

The 99th atom was named after Einstein. It is called Einsteinium. Einsteinium is a man-made metal that quickly breaks into smaller, simpler atoms.

• You are given an ounce of Einsteinium. Make up a description of what it looks like. Give it special properties and imagine what you could do with it.

Famous Einstein Quotes

The important thing is not to stop questioning.

I have no special gift. I am only passionately curious.

Charles Drew

Blood Scientist

Born: 1904 in Washington, D.C.   Lived to be 45 years old

Young Charles Drew

Charles was the oldest of five children. His dad installed carpets for a living. His mother was a school teacher.

Young Charles excelled in athletics. By the age of eight, he had won four swimming medals. In high school he starred in football, basketball, baseball and track. He was the most valuable player as a halfback on his college football team.

Young Drew never let athletics interfere with his studies. His grades and his athletic ability won him a scholarship to Amherst College. He was only one of 16 African American students at Amherst.

Why Dr. Drew Was Famous

After a few years of teaching biology, he decided to become a doctor. He went to Canada where he studied under a professor working on blood transfusions. As an intern, Dr. Drew saved a man's life with a blood transfusion.

Blood transfusions were not very common during the 1930s. Blood was hard to store. Giving the wrong blood to a patient could be fatal.

Dr. Drew's research led to blood that could be stored longer and was safer for patients. His idea involved separating **plasma** out of the blood. Plasma is a pale yellow fluid containing everything but blood cells or platelets. Look at the chart on the following page to you understand what blood is made of.

TLC10436 Copyright © Teaching & Learning Company, Carthage, IL 62321-001

Blood Chart

```
                              ┌──────── Blood ────────┐
        ┌──────────┬──────────┴──────────┬────────────┐
```

Plasma
Water,
sugar,
minerals,
protein

Red Cells
Carry
oxygen

**White
Cells**
Fight
germs

Platelets
Help
blood
to clot

Dr. Drew's blood research saved many lives during World War II. He set up blood banks in both England and the United States. The American Red Cross made him director of their blood donor project.

Dr. Drew spent the last years of his life training young doctors. Below is a quote that shows his attitude toward research.

There must always be the continuing struggle to make the increasing knowledge of the world bear fruit in increased understanding and the production of human happiness.

Appreciating Dr. Drew

Most sick people can be given plasma safely. Some patients require whole blood that contains both plasma and cells. A doctor must first know a patient's blood type before giving a transfusion. Mixing some kinds of blood can kill a patient. This is because some blood types clump when mixed.

The four basic blood types are shown in the table below.

Blood Types

Type	Can Get Blood From	Can Give Blood To
A	O, A	A, AB
B	O, B	B, AB
AB	A, B, AB, O	AB
O	O	A, B, AB, O

Do an experiment to show clumping, using milk and vinegar instead of blood.

- You'll need: milk, vinegar, a small glass and a tablespoon.
- Put two full tablespoons of milk in the glass.
- Add two full tablespoons of vinegar to the milk.
- Stir with the spoon for a few seconds.
- Wait a minute.

Examine the milk. Describe what happened to it.

What might happen if two wrong blood types were mixed?

LC10436 Copyright © Teaching & Learning Company, Carthage, IL 62321-0010

Observing Blood

Observe blood as Dr. Drew did in his lab.

- You'll need: a microscope and a glass slide.

- **Have an adult place a drop of blood on your slide.**

- Observe the drop under both low and high power.

- Try to find and identify the different blood cells. Use the chart below to help.

red

platelets   white

TLC10436 Copyright © Teaching & Learning Company, Carthage, IL 62321-001

Nobel Prize Winners
The World's Greatest Prize

Alfred Nobel was a Swedish chemist. He made a fortune making explosives with a substance called nitroglycerin. He hoped that it would be used for peaceful purposes such as mining and bridge building. Instead his explosives were mainly used in war.

To encourage peace instead of war, Nobel established a peace prize. It is awarded every year to a person or group that contributes the most toward world peace.

Nobel also established prizes for merit in physics, chemistry, physiology and medicine. Each winner gets a gold medal and up to a million dollars. The prizes are presented each year in Stockholm, Sweden.

Congratulations! You have just been awarded the Nobel Prize for your discovery of a new planet inhabited only by monkeys. Write a one-page acceptance speech to deliver at the party in Stockholm.

Nobel Winner Rosalyn Yalow

Born: 1921 in New York City

Dr. Yalow won the Nobel Prize for physiology and medicine in 1977. She was the first American woman to win the Nobel Prize in science.

As a young girl, her teachers encouraged her to make a career in science. Very few women in her time studied in the field of physics. Dr. Yalow applied her physics knowledge to research in medicine. She developed new ways to analyze blood and other body fluids.

Famous Quote from Yalow

I am a scientist because I love investigation.

Nobel Winner Luis Alvarez

Born: 1911 in San Francisco, California

Dr. Alvarez won the Nobel Prize for physics in 1968. His experiments involved the atoms that make up our world. He developed ways of speeding up atomic particles. Dr. Alvarez invented the bubble chamber that enabled scientists to observe the paths of invisible particles.

Fellow scientists called Dr. Alvarez the "prize wild-idea man." He has 22 patents in his name. He helped develop radar that keeps planes flying safely. He worked on the atom bomb. One patent was for a device that improves a person's golf game.

Dr. Alvarez was interested in everything. He invented a system that looked "through" the Egyptian pyramids to locate secret burial chambers. He studied dinosaurs and came up with a theory that a giant meteorite destroyed them 65 million years ago.

Dr. Alvarez Challenge

Could you create a different theory to explain why dinosaurs died out? Use your imagination and sense of humor.

Nobel Winner Richard Feynman

Born: 1918 in New York City

Dr. Feynman won the Nobel Prize in physics in 1965. His specialty was using complicated math to explain an atom's particles. He was a super teacher whose students followed him around from class to labs to his home. His lectures might include a practical joke or a session on his drums.

Dr. Feynman was gifted in many areas. As a joke he would break into locked safes. He was able to translate writings from ancient Mayan ruins.

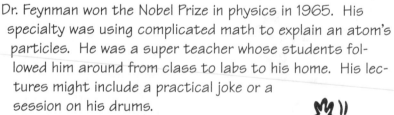

Above all, Dr. Feynman saw humor in everything.

TLC10436 Copyright © Teaching & Learning Company, Carthage, IL 62321-00

Dr. Feynman Challenge

1. Dr. Feynman's students wrote poems about him. Write a short poem about your favorite scientist.

2. Dr. Feynman actually took the number test below. There are six number twos mixed in with a lot of number fives. He found all the twos in five seconds. Time how fast you can find them.

3. Below is a diagram. It has 15 quadrilaterals. A quadrilateral is any figure with exactly four sides. How many can you find?

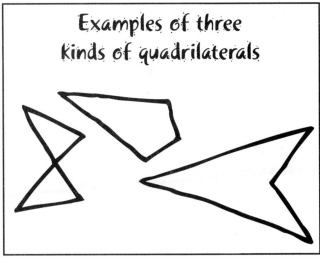

Examples of three kinds of quadrilaterals

Famous Quote from Feynman

If it disagrees with the experiment, it is wrong.

Scientist Research Project

This book is about great scientists and how they improved our lives. It has featured fewer than 20 of the great scientists. Many more scientists have contributed to our knowledge and well being.

Research a scientist on your own. Choose a scientist from the list below, or try finding your own scientist at the library or on the internet. Contact a local college for a scientist on their staff. Maybe you have a friend or family member who is a scientist. The scientist you research does not have to be someone world famous.

Use this outline for your research. Make your report interesting.

  A. What is your scientist's name?
  B. What country is he or she from?
  C. When was he or she born?
  D. What was your scientist's greatest accomplishment?
  E. What honors did he or she receive?
  F. What is the most interesting thing about your scientist?
  G. Include photos or drawings if possible.

Great Scientists List

Aristotle: Greek (384-322 B.C.)
Father of biology. First scientist to make accurate observations of nature.

James Audubon: American (1785-1851)
Naturalist who studied and drew detailed bird pictures.

Niels Bohr: Danish (1885-1962)
Theory of atomic structure involving electron shells.

Tycho Brahe: Danish (1602-1680)
Astronomer who made important observations and measurements without use of a telescope.

Luther Burbank: American (1849-1943)
Scientist who bred new types of plants.

Scott Carpenter: American (1925-)
Astronaut and aquanaut.

George Washington Carver: American (1864-1943)
Chemist who developed new products from peanuts.

Nicolaus Copernicus: German, Polish (1473-1543)
Astronomer who said the sun, not the Earth, was the center of the solar system.

Marie Curie: Polish (1867-1934)
Physicist who discovered radium and worked with radioactivity.

John Dalton: British (1766-1844)
Chemist who developed the early theory that all matter consists of atoms.

Charles Darwin: British (1804-1882)
Biologist who developed the theory of evolution. Sailed around the world collecting data on life evolution.

Leonardo Da Vinci: Italian (1452-1519)
Scientist and artist who drew plans for many modern inventions.

Charles Drew: American (1904-1950)
Biologist who developed new blood techniques including blood bank procedures.

Thomas Edison: American (1847-1931)
Invented incandescent light and many other useful items.

Albert Einstein: German, American (1879-1955)
Mathematician who developed math physics. Worked out mathematical theories involving relativity and the atom. Developed the formula $E = MC^2$.

TLC10436 Copyright © Teaching & Learning Company, Carthage, IL 62321-0010

Paul Erlich: German (1854-1915)
Bacteriologist who discovered how to stain bacteria to make them more visible.

Gabriel Fahrenheit: German (1686-1736)
Physicist who invented the alcohol and mercury thermometers.

Michael Faraday: British (1791-1867)
Physicist who worked in electronics.

Philo Farnsworth: American (1906-1971)
Invented the television picture tube.

Enrico Fermi: Italian, American (1901-1954)
Developed a method of obtaining power from an atomic pile.

Alexander Fleming: British (1881-1955)
Bacteriologist who discovered penicillin.

Benjamin Franklin: American (1706-1790)
Politician and scientist who experimented with lightning.

Galileo Galilei: Italian (1564-1642)
Father of modern science. Developed the modern experimental method. Worked on astronomy and gravity.

Robert Goddard: American (1882-1942)
Developed rocket science.

Jane Goodall: English (1934-)
Wildlife scientist.

Alice Hamilton: American (1869-1970)
Medical scientist.

William Harvey: Irish (1578-1657)
Discovered circulation of blood.

Hippocrates: Greek (450-377 B.C.)
Father of modern medicine.

Edwin Powell Hubble: American (1889-1953)
Astronomer.

Edward Jenner: English (1749-1823)
Developed the original smallpox vaccine.

Johanes Kepice: German (1571-1630)
Early astronomer.

Robert Koch: German (1843-1910)
Bacteriologist who discovered tuberculosis.

Antoine Lavoisier: French (1743-1794)
Father of modern chemistry. Developed the theory of how things burned combined with oxygen.

Anton Leeuwenhoek: Dutch (1632-1723)
Developed a microscope that enabled him to see bacteria.

Carolus Linnaeus: Swedish (1708-1778)
Discovered taxonomy, the science of classification.

Joseph Lister: English (1827-1912)
Founder of antiseptic surgery.

Guglielmo Marconi: Italian, American (1874-1937)
Developed the radio.

Margaret Mead: American (1901-1972)
Anthropologist who studied primitive societies and applied findings to modern society.

Gregor Mendel: Austrian (1822-1884)
Discovered the basic laws of heredity.

Albert Michelson: American (1852-1931)
Measured the speed of light.

Lisa Mitner: (1878-1968)
Nuclear physicist.

John Muir: American (1838-1914)
Famous conservationist.

Isaac Newton: British (1642-1727)
Discovered the laws of gravity.

Alfred Nobel: Swedish (1833-1896)
First to make dynamite. Established the famous science and peace prizes.

Louis Pasteur: French (1822-1895)
Discovered the germ theory. Developed the rabies vaccine.

Ivan Pavlov: Russian (1849-1936)
Did psychological experiments with dogs. Discovered the theory of conditioned reflex.

Auguste Piccard: Swiss (1884-1962)
Explored the upper atmosphere with balloons.

Joseph Priestly: British (1738-1804)
Discovered oxygen.

Ptolemy: Egyptian (About 130 A.D.)
Had the false theory that the Earth was the center of the universe.

Ernest Rutherford: British (1871-1937)
Studied radioactivity and atomic structure. Discovered Alpha and Beta rays.

Florence Rena Sabin: American (1871-1953)
Public health scientist.

Glen Seaborg: American (1912-1999)
Discovered many of the new atoms beyond number 92.

Harold Urey: American (1893-1981)
Help develop the atomic bomb. Discovered heavy hydrogen.

James Van Allen: American (1914-)
Discovered Earth's radiation belts.

Andreas Vesalius: Belgium (1514-1564)
Among the first to dissect a human body to discover how it works.

Women Scientists

Girls were not encouraged to become scientists many years ago. Things are different now. Many science colleges have close to 50% female students.

Here are a few women who led the way.

Margaret Mead

Anthropologist

Born: 1901 in Philadelphia, Pennsylvania
Lived to be 76 years old

Margaret was an anthropologist. Anthropology is the science that deals with people and their customs and cultures. The people studied may be modern or primitive.

Young Margaret was raised in a very intellectual home. Her dad was a college professor. Her mother was a sociologist. Their home was the meeting place for many brilliant people who exposed young Margaret to many new ideas.

School was not easy for Margaret, because she was much more advanced than most children. Her grandmother helped school her at home.

Later she attended Barnard College and was swept up in college life. She even became a member of a girl's club called the Ash Can Cats.

While she was a graduate student, she had a chance to study native tribes on the island of Samoa. She was intrigued by the role of young girls in Samoan society. She observed and collected data. This became the basis for her book called *Coming of Age in Samoa*. It made her famous. She wrote more than 30 other books.

TLC10436 Copyright © Teaching & Learning Company, Carthage, IL 62321-0010

Margaret Mead Activity

When Margaret was only eight years old, her dad asked her to observe and record her younger sister's speech patterns. Later, as an anthropologist, she spent years observing and collecting data on primitive people.

Now it is your turn to play anthropologist. Find a four- to seven-year-old child. Observe him or her carefully and patiently for at least half an hour. Record the 10 most interesting things the child does.

1. _____

2. _____

3. _____

4. _____

5. _____

6. _____

7. _____

8. _____

9. _____

10. _____

Famous Quote from Mead

Children are our vehicle for survival—for in them there is hope.

Sally Ride
Scientist in Space

Born: 1951 in Los Angeles, California   Still living

Young Sally excelled at both school and sports. She had to decide between professional tennis and science as a career. Science won. She earned her Ph.D. in physics at Stanford University. Then someone showed her an ad for NASA. They were looking for scientists to be trained as astronauts. There were 8000 applications sent to NASA. Sally was one of only 35 that were chosen.

She did well at astronaut school and became the first American woman to go into space. She flew in the *Challenger* space shuttle in both 1983 and 1984. Dr. Ride spent 343 hours floating in space.

Dr. Ride has won many awards. She was inducted into the Astronaut Hall of Fame in 2003. She has written four children's books including one called *To Space and Back*.

Dr. Ride carried out many science experiments while in space. Here is an experiment about air pressure and flying that she would have enjoyed.

- You'll need: a light ball and a hair dryer.
- Point the dryer **straight up**.
- Set the heat as **low as possible. Do not burn yourself**.
- Place the blower on medium or high.
- Carefully place the ball about 6" above the hair dryer and turn it loose.

What happened to the ball?

What happens to the ball if you slowly move the dryer to the right or left?

Dr. Ride would tell you that you have just demonstrated **Bernoulli's Principle**. That principle explains how airplanes can fly. It is based upon the fact that as air speeds up, it's pressure goes down.

Observation Time

- Look up Bernoulli and study his principle, then explain why the ball remained suspended above the dryer.

TLC10436 Copyright © Teaching & Learning Company, Carthage, IL 62321-0010

Chieng-Shiung Wu

Immigrant Scientist

Born: 1912 in Shanghai, China   Lived to be 84 years old.

Dr. Wu was born at a time in China when education was only for men. Her father recognized how special she was. He enrolled her in a class taught by a famous Chinese scholar. The scholar was also impressed by her genius. He found a way to enroll her in the University of Nanjing, where she majored in science.

Dr. Wu immigrated to the United States when she was 24. She earned a Ph.D. in physics at the University of California at Berkeley. She later went to Columbia University where she spent 37 years dedicated to science research.

Her specialty was atomic particles. Dr. Wu spent her later years doing medical research on sickle cell anemia.

Dr. Wu received many honors. She became the first female president of the American Physicists Society.

Here is a language challenge at which Dr. Wu would have excelled. It will make you appreciate how hard it was for her to study as an immigrant in our country. Could you study science at a Chinese university?

Observe the graceful Chinese characters for beauty, courage and peace.

Beauty

Courage

Peace

• Pick a favorite from the above. Try to duplicate it.

• Make up a Chinese character for health.

• Make up a Chinese character for your last name.

Young Scientists

Young People in Science

Many great scientists showed their talent early in life. It is never too early to start becoming a scientist. Entering a science fair is a good start. You may not win, but you will learn these skills that scientists need:

1. Observing carefully.
2. Following directions.
3. Measuring carefully.
4. Making intelligent hypotheses. (A hypothesis is a guess.)
5. Experimenting safely.
6. Experimenting until you succeed.

Reaching for the Scientific Stars

There are many science contests in which young people can participate. An adult may be able to help you enter one. A good place to start is the Craftsman/NSTA Inventors Contest. Craftsman is sold by Sears stores. NSTA stands for National Science Teachers Association. Here are some of their contest rules:

1. Students are challenged to use their imagination and mechanical ability to modify a common tool.
2. The contest is open to all students from grades 2 to 8.
3. Contestants must submit drawings and photos of their inventions.
4. Each contestant must also submit an inventor's log signed by an adult advisor.
5. Winners will receive up to $10,000 in United States Bonds. Their schools will receive extra prizes from Sears.

Here are some contest winning entries: a booster step and handle to help elderly people get into vans, a paintbrush handle that allows you to change the brush head, a sand timer that tells young children when to share toys.

TLC10436 Copyright © Teaching & Learning Company, Carthage, IL 62321-001

Invention Challenge

Can you invent a better type of tool or household gadget? Look around at all the tools and gadgets at home and school. How might you improve on the common hammer? Could you make a steel glove to drive in nails with your fist?

Could you make a device that helps blind, deaf or other handicapped people?

Could you use common objects such as straws or paper clips in a new and useful way?

Could you design a better chair, ladder or shovel?

- Start with observation and imagination.

- Free your mind to think creatively.

- Make full-size drawings of your project.

- Build the gadget and demonstrate it to your friends.

- Congratulate yourself! You are a young inventor.

Scientists in the Future

Science in the Past

Science has changed the way people live. It is hard to imagine our ancestors huddled in a dark, cold cave. Can you imagine life without electricity, cars or television?

Scientific inventions have changed our lives. The Chinese invented paper. Then someone invented the paper clip and stapler. Did you ever wonder who invented combs, scissors and haircuts?

Here are some inventions that changed the lives of your great-grandparents:

1865: Pasteur—safe milk

1876: Bell—telephone

1878: Edison—light bulb

1885: Benz—automobile

1886: Pemberton—Coca-Cola®

Can you list 10 more inventions that changed your great-grandparents' lives?

1. _____

2. _____

3. _____

4. _____

5. _____

6. _____

7. _____

8. _____

9. _____

10. _____

TLC10436 Copyright © Teaching & Learning Company, Carthage, IL 62321-001

Science Now

Scientists keep developing new and more awesome things. There are electric motors the size of a flea. There are windows that clean themselves and solar cells that power our homes.

Here are some inventions that changed your parents and grandparents' lives:

1902: Carrier—air conditioning

1924: Birdseye—frozen food

1928: Fleming—antibiotics

1977: Jobs and Wozniak—personal computer

1981: NASA—Space shuttle

Can you name 10 other important inventions that changed your parents and grandparents' lives?

1. _____

2. _____

3. _____

4. _____

5. _____

6. _____

7. _____

8. _____

9. _____

10. _____

LC10436 Copyright © Teaching & Learning Company, Carthage, IL 62321-0010

Science in the Future

Take a giant leap into the future to the year 2050. How old will you be? What do you predict life will be like in 2050? Use your imagination and sense of humor.

Choose any three future science topics below or add some of your own. Write a report on what you think those three areas will be like in 2050. Make sketches and models if possible.

1. Energy Sources
2. Food Sources
3. Pollution Solutions
4. Air, Sea and Land Transportation
5. Computers
6. Robots
7. Phones and Television
8. Money
9. Medicine and Health
10. World Population
11. Housing
12. Weather Control
13. Animal and Human Cloning
14. Space Travel

TLC10436 Copyright © Teaching & Learning Company, Carthage, IL 62321-00

Scientist Challenge

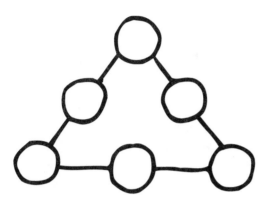

Magic Pyramid

For this pyramid can you place the numbers 1, 2, 3, 4, 5 and 6 in the circles shown on the left. Only one number may be placed in a circle and all numbers must be used. When the final arrangement is complete, the sum of each side's three numbers must all be the same number.

Frog Jump

A frog falls into a well that is 18 feet deep. Every day the frog jumps up a total distance of 6 feet. At night, as the frog grips the slimy well walls, it slips back down by 2 feet. At this rate, how many days will it take the frog to jump to the rim of the well?

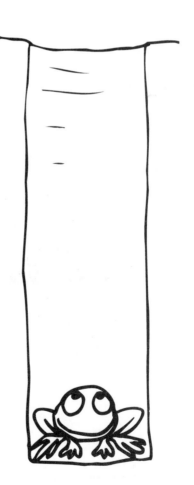

Scientist Challenge

Scientists love a challenge.
Here are some challenges for you.
Answers are on page 64.

Matching

Match the scientists to their discoveries.

1. Aristotle	A. Worked with radium
2. Galileo	B. Peanut discoveries
3. Newton	C. Electric lights
4. Einstein	D. Kites and lightning
5. Curie	E. Most ancient scientist
6. Pasteur	F. Airplanes
7. Franklin	G. Math genius
8. Edison	H. Experimented at Pisa
9. Carver	I. Germ theory of disease
10. Wright	J. Laws of motion

TLC10436 Copyright © Teaching & Learning Company, Carthage, IL 62321-00

Scientist Challenge

Scientists Scramble

The letters in each scientist's name are mixed up. Unscramble them. Answers are on page 64.

1. TOTELRISA

   _____

2. RUCIE

   _____

3. REVRAC

   _____

4. RAKFLINN

   _____

5. WONTEN

   _____

6. GLAELIO

   _____

7. THRWIG

   _____

8. STAPRUE

   _____

9. DESION

   _____

10. STINEENI

   _____

How Many Words?

How many words can you make from the scientists names below?
Each letter can be used more than once.

1. CARVER

2. NEWTON

3. ARISTOTLE

4. Your last name

Answer Key

Aristotle's Favorite Experiments, page 6

1. 16
2. The coin could not have BC on it. The coin was made *before* Christ was born.
3. The box must be four feet deep.

Fun with Math, page 43

1. Left Block: 15 blocks. Right Block: 14 blocks.
2.

8	1	6
3	5	7
4	9	2

3. Move top right of 9 to make a + out of the minus sign. You now have 12 + 3 = 15.

$$12+3=15$$

Magic Pyramid, page 61

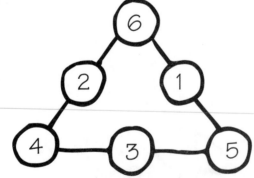

Frog Jump, page 61

It will take the frog four days. During the first day, the frog jumps up six feet and at night slides down two feet. The frog begins day 2 at the height of four feet, jumps to 10 feet but slides back two feet to eight feet. On day 3, the frog jumps to 14 feet, but slides back to 12 feet. On day 4, the frog jumps to 18 feet and leaves the well.

Matching, page 62

1. E.
2. H.
3. J.
4. G.
5. A.
6. I.
7. D.
8. C.
9. B.
10. F.

Scientists Scramble, page 63

1. Aristotle
2. Curie
3. Carver
4. Franklin
5. Newton
6. Galileo
7. Wright
8. Pasteur
9. Edison
10. Einstein

TLC10436 Copyright © Teaching & Learning Company, Carthage, IL 62321-0010